Tony Strachan is a writer, theatre director, choreographer and designer with a mosaic of performance experience over 25 years. His work ranges from writings for the intimacy of small stages to directing large-scale public performance concepts.

Tony's published writing credits include *State of Shock*, performed at Belvoir St, Playbox, Toe Truck and Riverina Theatre Company; *The Harlequin Shuffle* for Stage Company in South Australia; and *The Eyes of the Whites*, produced at Nimrod. He has written four plays for ABC Radio over the years and has been a writer-in-residence for Troupe in Adelaide, Toe Truck in Sydney and the Murray River Performing Group in Albury where he wrote a large-cast musical about debutante rituals called *Deb You Do, Deb You Don't*.

He has written and/or directed for Australian Theatre of the Deaf (*Tunnel Vision* and *The Sign is Right*), Sidetrack, Human Veins Theatre and Jigsaw in ACT, Death Defying Theatre, ABC Radio and the Festival of the Dreaming. He is founder and director of the long-standing outdoor troupe, Chrome, seen around the world at theatre festivals and events. He ran the outdoor components of the 1994 Melbourne and 1986 Adelaide Festivals.

Tony is presently Artistic Director of Australian Theatre of the Deaf.

Trisha Morton-Thomas as Mrs Jenny Bob in the 1999 Riverina Theatre
Company production. (Photo: Lee Verrall)

STATE OF SHOCK

Tony Strachan

Currency Press • Sydney

CURRENCY PLAYS

First published in 1986
by Currency Press Pty Ltd,
PO Box 2287, Strawberry Hills, NSW, 2012, Australia
enquiries@currency.com.au
www.currency.com.au

This revised edition published in 2000.

Reprinted in 2001, 2003, 2008, 2017

Cataloguing-in-publication data for this title is available from the National Library of Australia website: www.nla.gov.au

Typeset by Dean Nottle for Currency Press.
Cover design by Kate Florance.
Cover shows Lee Willis as Eddie and Trisha Morton-Thomas as Doreen in the 1999 Riverina Theatre Company production. (Photo: Lee Verrall).

Currency Press acknowledges the Traditional Owners of the Country on which we live and work. We pay our respects to all Aboriginal and Torres Strait Islander Elders, past and present.

Contents

Dedicated to the memory of Deidre Gilbert

FOREWORD

At the 1984 Playwrights' Conference I directed a workshop of Tony Strachan's play, *State of Shock.* The workshop involved Alma de Groen as dramaturg and its five actors were Ernie Dingo, Annie Saward, Lorraine Mafi-Williams, Robert Essex and John Stone. All of these people contributed enormously to the play's development.

The play seemed to me in some ways structurally unsatisfying, but as with Tony's *Eyes of the Whites,* which we did at the Nimrod in 1981, it had emotional power that developed gradually and finally drove the play to its climax. The heart of this play beats strongly.

It was seeing Percy Mtaa and Nbongeni Ngema in W*oza Albert!* in 1985 that lead me to suggest to Tony that he might consider a version of *State of Shock* for two actors, where its less satisfactorily naturalistic scenic development would be abandoned for a concentration on shared and dramatic storytelling. Two Aboriginal actors, cast perhaps closest to Eddy and Jenny Bob (on whom the play finally settles), would share between them all of the play's characters.

There were dangers involved in such an undertaking. A show like *Woza Albert!* is the result of years of shared performance experience, where a mutual understanding between the actors and a way of working had been developed before the show was even conceived. The show itself grew organically out of those two performers tackling an idea and developing the script, rather than beginning with a script and adapting it to their own purposes.

Moreover, such an approach to *State of Shock* would throw enormous demands on the two actors—demands requiring highly-developed skills of characterisation and agility of impersonation. The opportunities for Aboriginal actors to develop such skills on professional stages had been scarce up to that time. One of the reasons I looked to Western Australia when casting *State of Shock,* was that over a period of five years or so, with the collaboration of Andrew Ross and the playwright Jack Davis, Western Australia had stood out as the only place where there had been a continuing and developing tradition of professional Aboriginal theatre (outside of what was then known as the Aboriginal and Islander Dance Theatre).

While this experiment with *State of Shock* involved difficulties, it also threw up unexpected results. The character of O'Connor, for instance, was always, I thought, a somewhat uneasy mixture of cartoon and reality. Looking at the character as interpreted through Aboriginal eyes, he was distanced and planted firmly in satirical context. During the rehearsal period we saw the complexities of the character start to emerge and the satirical shell start to crack and reveal a real human centre. Such discoveries proved to be rich rewards for our experimental approach.

The major aim of the experiment, however, was to give an unalloyed clarity to the narrative. In creating theatre we are telling stories about ourselves: we put our lives and our society on stage as a way of seeing them clearly. It was precisely the simplicity of this idea that informed that first production of *State of Shock* back in 1986: two storytellers in a public space enacting a tale for an audience.

Neil Armfield

INTRODUCTION

I first discovered *State of Shock* in 1994 when I wrote and implemented the performing arts course at the Eora Aboriginal Visual and Performing Arts College in Redfern. I had previously used the TV documentary about Alwyn Peter, on whose life and trial the play is based, as part of my lectures on contemporary Aboriginal studies. Although the play had been written for two actors to play five roles, I used five students. It was a very interesting experiment.

In 1999 David Fenton, Artistic Director of the Riverina Theatre Company, asked me if I would direct a production of *State of Shock* under the aegis of the partnership the theatre had recently formed with Tandanya, the National Aboriginal Cultural Institute, in Adelaide. On reading the play again I realised that in the decade or so since Tony Strachan had written the play, on the one hand politically speaking many things had changed, on the other hand socially many things were the same, and in some instances conditions for Aboriginals were worse. For example, the number of young Aboriginals in gaols had risen—as had deaths in custody. Drink related violence in many communities was still a big problem.

Many people still do not understand the importance of the land in Aboriginal culture and the disastrous impact on contemporary Aboriginal life caused by being removed from our land and birth rights. Tony's play deals with these issues in a succinct and eloquent manner. The message within the play is, I believe, even more pertinent today than when it was first written.

I decided to direct the play using three actors in five roles. We had no costumes (the actors performed in their own clothes) and no set (simply a black box and a bed), just some essential props. Lighting was by Joe Mercurio and Sarah De Jong designed a wonderful soundscape. With Tony's permission I made some slight adjustments to the text to eliminate any caricature of Bernie, the non-Aboriginal reserve manager, and of the Lawyer—both played by Jim Holt. Trisha Morton-Thomas, a student of mine at Eora who had previously played Mrs Jenny Bob, played both Doreen and Mrs Jenny Bob. Lee Willis played Eddie. Performances were planned for Wagga Wagga, Griffith and Adelaide.

While we were rehearsing, I was asked to take the members of the Sydney Leadership Program for a day of Aboriginal Cultural studies. During the course of my talks I told them about the play and how it dealt with many of the problems facing Aboriginals today. I invited the group to watch a rehearsal the following week. They were 'shocked' by what they had seen and asked if the play would have a Sydney season. When I said there was not enough money, they set about collecting $26,000. With the help of Ros Horin, Artistic Director at the Griffin Theatre Company, together with other members of the Leadership Program, the play had a very successful run at the Stables Theatre in Sydney in June 1999. It was a tremendous and stimulating opportunity to expose this powerful play to a new generation of theatregoers.

Noel Tovey

AUTHOR'S NOTE

This play was originally conceived as a work for five actors. The script as it appears between these covers is for the two-hander version of 1986. However, it is easily possible to adapt the play for any number of actors up to five. If more than two actors are used, the role of man and woman can be shared with the additional actors. This may require a rewritten version of those monologues, particularly if the extra actors are white. If using the two-actor version, one should engage two Aboriginal actors, preferably a young man and a mature woman. The man's principal role is Eddie Thomas. The woman's principal role is Mrs Jenny Bob. Both actors play Doreen Simpson and Bernie O'Connor at different times. The woman plays the lawyer.

In the scenes where three characters appear, swift role transferral occurs, but generally no description of the mechanics of this is included in the stage directions. At those points in the play where the two actors drop character and speak formally to the audience they have been described as Man and Woman.

The scenes are performed within an informal storytelling framework. The actors begin by developing a rapport with the audience. They introduce themselves as actors, talk about the characters in the play and prepare them for the role-sharing approach. Finally they explain the true story from which the play draws its inspiration: that of Alwyn Peter who stabbed his girlfriend Deidre Gilbert in December 1979 and went before the Brisbane Supreme Court in September 1981. At other places in the performance of the play, the actors break character and communicate directly with the audience using a mixture of hymns, songs, personal stories and parts of the Alwyn Peter trial transcript. No attempt has been made to depict that linking material in these pages.

Tony Strachan

In Queensland there have been created communities in which the incidence of homicide and very serious assaults is among the highest recorded and published in the world. To be a member of such a community one does not have to be mad or bad. One only has to be Aboriginal.

Defence lawyer Des Sturgess, in his opening address in the trial of Alwyn Peter, 1982

Our Aborigines live like kings. They are on clover.

Queensland Premier, Sir Joh Bjelke Petersen, quoted in the press the same month

The author wishes to thank Alwyn Peter and his family for their advice and encouragement, and Missus Jean Jimmy for the inspiration she supplied.

State of Shock was originally presented as a staged reading at the Australian National Playwrights Conference, Canberra, in May 1984 with Ernie Dingo, Lorraine Mafi-Williams, Annie Saward, John Stone and Robert Essex, and was directed by Neil Armfield.

This revised version of the text was first performed at the Belvoir Street Theatre, Sydney, on 27 August 1986 with the following cast:

Lynette Narkle
Ernie Dingo

Directed by Neil Armfield
Designed by Stephen Curtis and Rosie Boylan
Lighting design by Neil Simpson

Toe Truck Theatre restaged the play for schools touring in 1989 in a production directed by Alison Summers, with actors Lydia Miller and Raymond Blanco.

The play was again produced by Riverina Theatre Company in 1999, and opened at the Riverina Playhouse in Wagga Wagga on 17 February. It subsequently travelled to the Tandanya Centre in Adelaide and the Stables Theatre in Sydney. The cast was:

Trisha Morton-Thomas
Lee Willis
Jim Holt

Direction and Design Conception, Noel C. Tovey
Set and Costume Design, Andrew Raymond
Lighting Design, Joseph Mercurio
Sound Design, Sarah de Jong

CHARACTERS

EDDIE THOMAS, in his early 20s
DOREEN SIMPSON, in her late teens
MRS JENNY BOB, Eddie's grandmother, in her 60s
BERNIE O'CONNOR, a public servant, in his mid-50s
LAWYER, in his 30s

SETTING

Scenes in Act One are played out in and around Cheka Aboriginal Reserve in the far north of Queensland.

In the second act, two of the scenes take place in Townsville's Stuart Creek Prison.

The events of the play take place in the present.

Whilst this play was inspired by an event which actually occurred, the characters are not intended to portray any person alive or dead. Any resemblance to any person is coincidental.

ACT ONE

SCENE ONE

The Reserve. Daytime. DOREEN *and* EDDIE *walk in side by side. She is swinging a billycan.*

DOREEN: You smilin'.

EDDIE: No I'm not.

DOREEN: I had a mirror I'd show you. Y'are. You always smile out the bush.

> *They stop. He looks back.*

EDDIE: Cheka Reserve look pretty small, don't it?

DOREEN: You been back three weeks and you never told me 'bout Townsville, Eddie.

EDDIE: Couldn't see much from inside.

DOREEN: You bin see it when you got out.

EDDIE: Yeh. Busy place that one. They got a lotta things. Tall houses, lotsa cars and shops, lotta lights. One thing they ain't got, they ain't got our giant tip trucks. [*Indicating in the distance*] None of them in Townsville. Or Cairns.

DOREEN: No dust, eh?

EDDIE: Look at that one go. Like a tribe of Indians galloping. And now it's the cavalry chasing them.

DOREEN: What's a cavalry, Eddie?

EDDIE: American soldiers. You seen 'em. In that John Wayne movie last Christmas.

DOREEN: Oh, yeah. That fella shot a lot of Indians.

EDDIE: You know, company's diggin' up a new place now. Before I went to Townsville they were over there.

DOREEN: Make a circle soon.

EDDIE: Cavalry closin' in.

DOREEN *opens the billy.*

DOREEN: Look what I made. Samwich.

EDDIE: Where's the damper?

DOREEN: Bread 'n Vegemite.

> *She hands him one. He takes a bite.*

All right?

EDDIE: Not bad.

DOREEN: You heard from Bill or Andy?

EDDIE: They still in Cairns.

DOREEN: Drinkin' on the beach.

EDDIE: That's m'brothers.

DOREEN: You should tell them to come back to Cheka.

EDDIE: Okay. I'll send 'em the ticket money. Got it there?

> DOREEN *puts her hand in her dress as though pulling out a wad of notes. She slaps his hand.*

DOREEN: There y'are.

> *They laugh.*

EDDIE: Your mum still sick, eh?

> *She nods.*

She see the Sister?

DOREEN: Last week. But she loss the pills. She 'fraid to go back.

EDDIE: She want to die?

> DOREEN *shakes her head.*

So tell 'er to go back.

DOREEN: I tried.

EDDIE: I'll tell 'er.

DOREEN: She won't for sure, then. She don't like you. You fight the Island boys.

EDDIE: That friendly fightin', eh?

DOREEN: Lump a wood across the head? He's in hospital, that boy. Two weeks, they reckon.

EDDIE: What you worried about him for?

DOREEN: He friend of the family. I know him since I bin little.

EDDIE: You like him then, eh?

DOREEN: I don't like him.

EDDIE: But you still talkin' to 'im, and he's an Islander.

DOREEN: Our dads bin good mates when we kids.

EDDIE: Sure. He was the one who broke my rib that time at the pub, so he asked for that lump a wood, eh?

DOREEN: Boolimun get you one day.

EDDIE: I be all right. My cousin's police... Nice sandwich, that one.

DOREEN: Here.

She hands him another.

EDDIE: Know how they made this Vegemite?

DOREEN: Nuh.

EDDIE: Them blackfellas see them white settlers comin' with guns, scared 'em. Black skin just drop off, on the ground. Blackfella gone, whitefella pick 'em up, take it and melt it down and make Vegemite. There weren't no massacres. Those whitefellas frightened us black fellas into turning white.

DOREEN: Is this true...?

EDDIE: No.

DOREEN: Eddie, I never know when to believe you, humbug. What's that story mean? Eddie, what's it mean?

EDDIE: Nothin'. Nice sandwich.

DOREEN: That's bad story.

EDDIE: That's what I told that Islander before I hit him with the timber.

DOREEN: He told you this?

EDDIE picks his teeth.

You fight too much. You gotta stop.

EDDIE: Them grass roots there. Y'pull 'em up and cut off the bottom and cook with the fish. Pop reckons.

DOREEN: You work soon, and we get some ticket to go away to Brissie.

EDDIE: He says that tree over there five hundred years old. Some over home in Yambala even older. Old people, those trees, what d'y'reckon?

DOREEN: We can live in house, with nice bathroom.

EDDIE: I listened to one old tree in Yambala, and I could hear it talkin'.

DOREEN: We have washing machine.

EDDIE: 'Nother lingo.

DOREEN: And a big white fridge.

EDDIE: But it was talkin'. Tree talk, eh?

DOREEN: You hear what I say?

EDDIE: Yeh.

DOREEN: Maybe company give you job.

EDDIE: Nah. Island boys get all the jobs now. They even driving them elephant trucks, couple of 'm.

> DOREEN *strokes his shoulder.*

DOREEN: This scar from fightin'?

> *He nods.*

I don't like you fightin' or gettin' angry. [*Pulling her own T-shirt up*] That's what I got from my husband's anger.

> *There is a scar on her back.*

EDDIE: You's all right now.

DOREEN: Nearly died but... Your body like an old tree. Marks everywhere.

EDDIE: Marks tell the story of a man's life.

DOREEN: You promise never smash louvre 'gain, eh? That glass cut you too much.

EDDIE: They changin' them louvres to tin now.

> *She strokes his arm.*

DOREEN: No need to think of other men. I told you so many time, I finish with my husband. I got no one but you. No husband, no Islander, just Eddie.

> *They hold each other's gaze.*

EDDIE: Come on.

DOREEN: Kiss a bit first.

EDDIE: A bit.

> *They kiss gently.* DOREEN *takes a flat, heart-shaped river stone from her pocket and hands it to* EDDIE.

DOREEN: For you.

EDDIE: [*reading*] 'To Eddie... from his girl Doreen, from her heart'... What's that?

DOREEN: Your beautiful face. I draw it with a nail.

EDDIE: Mmm. Good-lookin' fella, eh?

> *He pockets it. They hold each other.*

SCENE TWO

Back garden. Daytime. JENNY BOB *enters with washing in a bucket. She peers around, then calls to someone offstage.*

JENNY: Hey, Georgina, you see who took my line?

> DOREEN *enters.*

Doreen, my washing line's missing, pet.

DOREEN: It must have gone.

JENNY: Thanks.

DOREEN: It was here yes'dy. In the morning.

JENNY: That's a big help, Doreen.

DOREEN: And I seen it in the afternoon. Yes'dy.

JENNY: Yesterday is not today.

DOREEN: Must've gone for a ride with… ah…

JENNY: Eddie.

DOREEN: I din' say that.

JENNY: I wonder what he could have been doing with it?

DOREEN: Well…

JENNY: Yes.

DOREEN: They had a car. In the night.

JENNY: Where did that come from? Never mind.

DOREEN: It must've breaked down. Just over there.

JENNY: So they got a tow and used my washing line. That's true, I know it.

DOREEN: Maybe.

JENNY: No maybes about it. Out of sugar, washing line's gone and the drain's blocked again. I think it's my time to join the Heavenly Father.

DOREEN: Missus Jenny Bob—

JENNY: You call me Gran'ma, child.

DOREEN: Gran'ma, you the Chairman of Cheka Aborigine Council.

JENNY: I'm Chairlady, yes.

DOREEN: Well, Eddie need a jobs.

JENNY: A lot of people need jobs.

DOREEN: If you talk to company for a jobs, then he can work and make some money.

JENNY: The company got no jobs for Eddie.

DOREEN: Maybe you can talk to manager for a jobs in Reserve.

JENNY: This manager doesn't like Eddie.

DOREEN: What for?

JENNY: He thinks Eddie steals and fights and breaks the houses too much.

DOREEN: Only sometimes. When he get angry.

JENNY: Manager Taylor says prison has made Eddie worse.

DOREEN: Taylor got face like cement.

JENNY: He's got ulcers, poor fellow. He won't smile till they put him in the ground. Then maybe we'll get a new manager with some happiness in his heart.

DOREEN: Eddie and me, we's gonna go way somewheres.

JENNY: That's a good idea, child. Eddie's been talking about Yambala.

DOREEN: Maybe somewhere else like Brisbane...

JENNY: No troubles at Yambala. No bar. No cars. And they haven't even got 'round to mining it yet. You can stay with Eddie's mum and dad in the shack. What about your mum, Doreen, she still sick?

> DOREEN *nods*.

You should be home caring for her.

DOREEN: She tol' me to get out.

JENNY: She needs her daughters. What if she falls down and no one about? What'll she do then?

DOREEN: She sick womans, but she can sure scream like a big man.

JENNY: Your dad still not come back?

DOREEN: Nuh.

JENNY: When he was young at Yambala we called him the Black Fish. He'd go down in that sea and stay under and we thought he's never coming back. And, just when we deciding to have his funeral, up he comes with a turtle like this, and a lobster out like this, and half dozen prawns in his mouth. The Black Fish, that was your dad.

DOREEN: That true? I never seen him like that.

JENNY: That was before you came along. Before we got moved.

DOREEN: He real sick too, Gran'ma.

JENNY: I know, pet. Lots of sickness. You want a cup of tea?

> DOREEN *nods.*

I put the kettle on. [*Taking out some money*] You run over to the store for some sugar.

> DOREEN *takes the coins and exits.* JENNY BOB *picks up the washing, stands and spots something off.*

Where have you been? Send you off one day for a five-minute job and don't see you till the next.

> EDDIE *enters.*

Don't think I don't know why you didn't come back. Boolimun been sniffing 'round here like dogs all night.

EDDIE: They patrollin' the store as well, but I got in.

> *He produces a brown bag..*

JENNY: Ahh… You didn't forget your grandmother after all. I'll have two bags in a minute. Doreen's gone for another one. I want you to come here.

> EDDIE *fronts.*

I want my washing line back by tomorrow morning, hear?

EDDIE: Yeah.

JENNY: What you doing with a motor car, anyway?

EDDIE: Belonged to a friend.

JENNY: A friend you never met, most likely. The boolimun say you put an Islander in hospital. Did I raise you up to do such things? I suppose you were drinking.

> EDDIE *looks away.*

How can I be proud of you when you try to kill other people?

EDDIE: I didn't try to kill him.

JENNY: I got to go to Council meeting tonight. I got to sit with the other councillors. I got to look in their eyes and talk about ways to make this a peaceful place while the grandson I reared myself is the biggest troublemaker around.

EDDIE: I didn't want to hit him. My head ran away from my body that night.

JENNY: I know, my boy. But you got to hold onto your head or the boolimun will take you again, the courts will send you to Stuart, and I won't see you for another six months.

EDDIE: I won't make any more trouble, Gran'ma. I'll go to Yambala.

JENNY: That's good. Your mum and dad will be so happy. And I'll go up there and visit you. You take your girlfriend, eh?

EDDIE: Mum not keen on her.

JENNY: She will be. You take Doreen and show her your father's ground.

EDDIE: All right.

JENNY: All right. Now, see that bush?

He nods.

See this washing?

She picks up the bucket, thrusts it into his arms.

Shake the dust out of the bush first. [*She starts to leave, then stops and turns.*] My washing line. By tomorrow. Morning.

She exits. He looks into the bucket and over at the bush. DOREEN *enters with a bag of sugar.*

DOREEN: I ask your gran'ma if she see Mister Taylor 'bout a jobs.

EDDIE: He won't give me nothin'. I'm a black sheep.

DOREEN: You got to get a jobs, Eddie, so we can go 'way to Brissie.

EDDIE: No. We goin' to Yambala.

DOREEN: But there's no houses there. You say they all burned.

EDDIE: Don't need houses. You wanna be outside all the time up there. I'll take you to my special places. The place where the turtles make their eggs. The green cave where I hid when I was a kid. And I take you to the best lagoon you ever seen. Clear like glass, with tadpoles and white lillies and dragonflies. We sit down near the edge, at the feet of the old man with the initiation scar on his chest, old man who never move.

DOREEN: Who that old man?

Raymond Blanco as Eddie and Lydia Miller as Doreen in the 1989 Toe Truck Theatre production. (Photo: Chooi Tan)

EDDIE: Gum tree. Oldest silver gum in Cape York, I reckon. Got a mark from a knife in the middle of his body. That old man callin' me there right now.

DOREEN: Eddie, what if a wild pig have a go at me?

EDDIE: I can get Pop's twenty-two.

DOREEN: You got toilet paper up there?

EDDIE: Sure. It's green and grows everywhere. Stop worryin'.

She draws closer to him.

DOREEN: You protect me.

EDDIE: Yeah.

DOREEN: You hold me tight when the sun go away.

EDDIE: If you want.

DOREEN: An' tell me things.

EDDIE: I'll tell you the stories that old man tells me.

DOREEN: And when we come back, we get some money and go to Brisbane.

EDDIE: Might be. Might be.

DOREEN: Might be.

SCENE THREE

The edge of a football field on the Reserve. Daytime. O'CONNOR *stands with a golf club, frozen in a pose.*

MAN: This is Bernie O'Connor, boss of the DAI... that's the Department of Aboriginal Improvement. He wants to be a politician and is running for State election in six months. He's a bit sick of his job, you see, been in it for over twenty years. This fella gets up this way quite a lot, reckons he loves black people. Got a bit of a blood pressure problem. He's been told to take up golf. Got a nice swing, hasn't he? He better get a nice swing in the voting too or he hasn't got a hope.

O'CONNOR: Relax. Head loose. Hands loose. Legs loose. Grip... right little finger along left index finger. Concentrate. Bend the knees slightly. Control the swing... feels good... *Power!* [*He swings and hits the ball. It has obviously hooked badly. He glares down the fairway.*] You! Don't just stand there. I've told you, I hit it, you run. I *hit,* you *run!* [*Under his breath*] Stupid little monkey.

He places another ball on the ground. He positions himself in front of the ball. EDDIE *strolls on with a roll of masking tape and watches.*

Head loose. Hands loose. Legs apart. Bend, control, concentrate… *Power!*

He swings and walks forward, shading his eyes to look into the distance. He turns to EDDIE.

Can you see where that went?

EDDIE: Yeah.

O'CONNOR: Left or right of that stump?

EDDIE: It's between your legs, Mister O'Connor.

O'CONNOR *stares down and looks at it for a few moments. He peers down the fairway.*

O'CONNOR: Bloody caddy. [*Shouting*] You don't run *while* I'm hitting! I *hit,* you *don't* run!… You're sacked.

He picks up the ball.

EDDIE: Here's the sticky, Mister O'Connor. You got my dough there?

O'CONNOR: Where'd you put them?

EDDIE: All over.

O'CONNOR: Council Chambers? Store? I hope you put one up in the canteen… Up high? Those posters cost me a lot of money so I don't want them ripped down.

EDDIE: I stuck it on the ceiling.

O'CONNOR: Mmm. Now, that was three dollars, wasn't it?

EDDIE: Four.

O'CONNOR: Four?

EDDIE: Yeah.

O'CONNOR: You're a black Norm Gallagher, Mister Eddie Thomas.

He gives him the money.

What'll you do with it?

EDDIE: I'll buy ammo for the twenty-two.

O'CONNOR: A hunter, eh? Would you like to see a real gun?

EDDIE: Oh, yeah.

> O'CONNOR *takes a brand new, state-of-the-art piece from his golf bag. He hands it to* EDDIE.

O'CONNOR: What do you think?

EDDIE: Feel good in the shoulder.

O'CONNOR: That trigger action's something, isn't it?

EDDIE: Sure different to the twenty-two.

O'CONNOR: Those ducks won't have a chance.

EDDIE: You going shootin'?

O'CONNOR: Tomorrow morning, at the lagoon.

EDDIE: I know somewhere a lot better. Near Threeways.

> EDDIE *checks the telescopic sights.*

O'CONNOR: You offering to take me there?

EDDIE: Cost y'.

O'CONNOR: Cost me what?

EDDIE: Make an offer.

O'CONNOR: Ten.

EDDIE: Twenty.

O'CONNOR: Fifteen.

> *Pause.*

EDDIE: Have to get there early.

O'CONNOR: I'll pick you up at the gate at five-thirty sharp.

EDDIE: Okay. [*He sights down the barrel.*] You pretty good shot, eh?

O'CONNOR: Put it this way, I'm in the top three at Brisbane's finest rifle range.

EDDIE: But that a bit different from the bush, ain't it?

O'CONNOR: How's that?

EDDIE: Things in the bush they movin', wind blowing a little bit… Like that branch over there, see it, goin' up and down?

O'CONNOR: I could hit that branch.

EDDIE: Could y'?

O'CONNOR: You're damn right.

EDDIE: Okay. Go on.

O'CONNOR: Here, now?

EDDIE *holds out the rifle.*

You're implying I can't, aren't you?

EDDIE: Maybe we should bet on it.

O'CONNOR: You haven't got any money, son.

EDDIE: I got four dollars, and I got 'nother fifteen comin' tomorrer.

O'CONNOR: Okay.

O'CONNOR *takes ammunition from his golf buggy and loads. He sights the branch.*

EDDIE: So we bettin' nineteen dollars.

O'CONNOR: Yes… nineteen… says I… can hit that… branch.

He fires. They both peer out.

What's wrong with this thing?

EDDIE: I'm a rich man. Thirty-eight bucks.

O'CONNOR: Did you fiddle with the sights?

EDDIE: Nuh. I'll prove it, you give me a shot.

O'CONNOR: Now look here—

EDDIE: You get a chance to win your dough back.

O'CONNOR: You'll bet the nineteen on hitting the branch yourself?

EDDIE: No. Double or nothing. I'm puttin' my thirty-eight up front, eh?

O'CONNOR: All right. But don't you whinge when you miss. That's the safety catch.

EDDIE *aims and fires.*

Jesus!

EDDIE: Broke that branch clean off, eh?

O'CONNOR: Bloody Christ Almighty!

EDDIE: Hey, I's gettin' real close to the dole now. Thirty-eight 'n' thirty-eight, that's seventy-six bucks.

O'CONNOR: I'm not going to Threeways tomorrow so you can forget the fifteen. [*He takes out his wallet.*] Seventy-six minus fifteen… seventy-six away from… fifteen from… that's fifty-nine… sixty-three…

EDDIE: Sixty-nine.

O'CONNOR: I know! Sixty-nine. There's your money. Now scram.

EDDIE: You bet.

EDDIE *exits.* O'CONNOR *examines the telescopic sights, swearing under his breath.* JENNY BOB *enters.*

JENNY: What you think you doing, Mister Director? What you shooting this gun for? This is Aboriginal reserve, not the Wild West. Who do you think you are, Roy Rogers? You are a director, not a cowboy. What are all our childrens going to think of your behaviour? Eh?

He lowers the gun.

O'CONNOR: Why aren't the kids in their bloody classrooms?

JENNY: Some of them being caddies for a start.

They glare at each other.

O'CONNOR: If you'd been on time none of this would've happened. You're fifteen minutes late.

JENNY: Your time, maybe. But I's fifteen minutes early, blackfella time. Some people got no Volvo to get them 'round, only got their old legs… You going to drive your blood pressure right up, Director. I think you better calm down a bit before we talk.

O'CONNOR: I'm all right. I just got cheated by a black highwayman and a faulty gun.

JENNY: You know, I seen your face staring at me everywhere this morning.

O'CONNOR: I'm a political candidate.

JENNY: You have finally done it.

O'CONNOR: Yep. At last I'll get a chance to directly represent the people of the North.

JENNY: So you going to live up in your electorate, then?

O'CONNOR: No, no. I look on the North as my second home. I'll be of more use in Brisbane, close to the Parliament.

JENNY: But Queensland Parliament only meets fifteen days a year.

O'CONNOR: You're well-informed.

JENNY: I got my ear to the ground.

O'CONNOR: Well then, I suppose you've heard there's been a bit of hanky-panky going on about Yambala again.

JENNY: What do you mean?

O'CONNOR: Some of your family are there without the manager's permission.

JENNY: That's because I gave it to them.

O'CONNOR: You're supposed to have his approval too.

JENNY: They'd still be here if we waited for him. He's got a rubbish dump on his desk. He's like all you mob, likes his paper.

O'CONNOR: Joint approval must be arranged for a permit to be issued. I expect you as Chairwoman to abide by that rule.

JENNY: People ask me why aren't we free to go?

O'CONNOR: They're free, as long as they get the permit.

JENNY: Where were you born, Director?

O'CONNOR: Ipswich.

JENNY: Even though you live in Brisbane now, don't you go to Ipswich sometimes?

O'CONNOR: You know I do. I called in there on my way up.

JENNY: Did you get a permit from the Premier?

O'CONNOR: Of course not, damn it.

JENNY: So why must we get a permit to go to our home?

O'CONNOR: Every time I come up here, you get around to the same old pitch. Yambala is gone. It belongs to the mining company now. Every bush, every tree…

JENNY: Every mineral.

O'CONNOR: I do not understand you lot. You're a mere fifty miles from your home turf and you never stop moaning.

JENNY: It is true you don't understand. New Australians like you can be born in Ipswich, get your school in Melbourne, work in Brisbane, and have holidays every year on the Gold Coast. It has no meaning where you were born.

O'CONNOR: No, and that saves a hell of a lot of trouble. Can you imagine if every Australian asked us to stop land development so they could go and camp on the spot they were born every time they felt like it? The place'd be a bloody madhouse. Mineral exploration is essential for the future of this State, and sometimes people have to sacrifice one thing for another.

JENNY: What the other, Director?

O'CONNOR: A high standard of living for all Queenslanders.

JENNY: That what we got here?

O'CONNOR: What you've got here is better than ten years ago. And now I'm giving you the chance to improve things even further. By putting me in Parliament.

Lynette Narkle as Mrs Jenny Bob in the 1986 Belvoir St Theatre production. (Photo: Hugh Hamilton)

JENNY: Put you in a hole be best way to improve things 'round here.

They laugh.

O'CONNOR: Now there'll be some other candidates trying to get on the Reserve in the next few months. We don't want socialist stirrers running all over the place, do we? It only confuses people.

JENNY: Our people should hear what every candidate says, Director. That's democracy.

O'CONNOR: Someone's been at you already, by the sound of it.

JENNY: No. I read the Constitution.

O'CONNOR: I thought you didn't like paper.

JENNY: Some paper is all right. Like voting paper.

O'CONNOR: You're a smart operator, Jenny Bob, I'll give you that. 'Some paper is all right.' That's good. [*He laughs.*] I might be congratulating you on a new career shortly, mightn't I?

JENNY: What career you talking about?

O'CONNOR: Oh, this little offer you've had from the Land Rights Committee.

JENNY: How do you know about this?

O'CONNOR: Be interesting to see what you do about that offer. Yes indeed.

JENNY: They given me time to think about it.

O'CONNOR: Yes. A lot to think about too, I'd imagine. All that extra work, the interminable meetings, the travel. How are those old legs coping?

JENNY: I been standing beside you for ten minutes and I haven't fallen down.

O'CONNOR: Now don't get het-up about it. I'm one of your strongest supporters. As long as you act responsibly. And to prove how strongly I feel about you, I'm going to recommend an immediate start on the construction of a new house for you. All the doo-dads, proper bathroom, modern kitchen, and a laundry with a real washing machine. And up on stilts to keep those old feet high and dry in the wet.

JENNY: Director, if you going to spend the money, spend it on laundries and drains for all our old houses.

O'CONNOR: I thought you'd jump at the chance of a new house.

JENNY: I'd jump if we all got them. What will it mean to the people here if only I get one? It will mean I talked for myself.

O'CONNOR: I'm not going to argue with you in this mood but I do think you're entitled to a privilege or two.

JENNY: I can't stand 'round here talking all day. I got to do my duties. How long you going to stay with us?

> O'CONNOR *takes his car keys from a pocket.*

O'CONNOR: Just overnight.

JENNY: Why do you stay on reserves so much, Director? You think reserves nice places, or you just like to save your travel allowance?

O'CONNOR: Well, this way I can get close to the people, can't I? I'll be passing through again in a week too, you know. [*He starts the motor, puts his seat-belt on and winds down the press-button driver's window.*] I'll be looking forward to hearing what you decide about that job.

> *He revs the motor and drives off.* JENNY BOB *stands looking after him. She raises her eyes to the heavens.*

JENNY: Parliament. Lord have mercy on us.

SCENE FOUR

Night. JENNY BOB's *backyard.* DOREEN *conceals a screwdriver, hunting knife and a .22 rifle in different places. We hear someone approaching. She exits quickly.* EDDIE *appears from another direction shouting backwards.*

EDDIE: You black prick! You ain't no father, you fuckin' piece of shit! You hear me? The lot of you, all pricks!

> *He starts to search the space.* DOREEN *dances on as he discovers, and rips open, the Omo packet.*

Where's my hunting knife?

DOREEN: [*pointing at the Omo*] Gonna do y'washing? First time ever, I reckon.

EDDIE: Where's my knife?

DOREEN: How 'bout washing my undies too?

EDDIE: Where's my fuckin' knife?

DOREEN: How would I know?

EDDIE: Yeah, how would you know? You don't know nothin'.

DOREEN: That's right.

EDDIE: That's the trouble with you, you know nothin'! You got nothin'! You are nothin'!

DOREEN: I got somethin'. I got my head on my shoulders. Can't see yours nowheres.

EDDIE: [*shoving her*] I want my fuckin' knife, *now!*

DOREEN: What you gonna do with it, peel the potatoes?

EDDIE: Get it now, or I'll fuckin' kill you. Hear me? *Get it!*

She exits and returns with the .22

DOREEN: This be better for what you want to do, eh? This be lot easier to use on your dad. Then you can shoot your brothers and sisters and you mum and your grand'ma. And then you can put a bullet into me!

She thrusts it into his arms.

No, shoot me first, that be better. Shoot me. Go on. I's nothin', nothin' you reckon, so nothin' wrong with shootin' me. Right through the front here. Real easy for you... Come on, big man, *shoot!*

He stares at her, then turns away slowly.

Come away down the creek, come on, come on. I loves you.

He puts his hand over the end of the barrel.

Eddie!

He pulls the trigger. The rifle goes off.

SCENE FIVE

Night. The visitors' guesthouse. O'CONNOR *puts his suitcase down, goes to the window.*

O'CONNOR: Kids! Over here. Uncle Bernie's back. [*He takes several handfuls of lollies from his pocket and scatters them out through the window.*] Okay, off you go... More tomorrow. All finish now. When you get home, you tell your mums I'll take you away if they don't vote for me. Like the pourri-pourri man! [*He watches.*] Love those little black bastards.

There is a knock on the door. He opens it to DOREEN.

Hello.

DOREEN: Yes.

O'CONNOR: Tell me your name, then.

DOREEN: Doreen.

O'CONNOR: Doreen. Come in. I'm Mister O'Connor, but I imagine you already know that.

DOREEN: Yes.

O'CONNOR: You look a bit shy. Do your parents know you're here, Doreen?

She shakes her head.

I'm not a crocodile. I won't bite. Come and sit over here. You must be very young.

DOREEN: I's eighteen.

O'CONNOR: And what was on your mind, Doreen?

Pause.

DOREEN: You can get a jobs.

O'CONNOR: Job for you?

She shakes her head.

For your father? Brother?

DOREEN: Friend.

O'CONNOR: Your boyfriend?

She nods.

You'd like a job for your boyfriend.

She nods again. He holds out a lolly.

Here you are.

She pockets it.

And what sort of job does your boyfriend want?

DOREEN: Drive big truck for company. Please.

O'CONNOR: Doreen, the company doesn't like giving jobs to Cheka Aboriginals because they go walkabout too much.

Pause.

DOREEN: I bin see papers all 'round with your picture, and all peoples here they reckon you gonna be top boss in Parliament. An' I reckon you be doing anything you want 'round here, so I comin' to ask for jobs.

O'CONNOR: Cheka people are saying that, are they?

She nods.

DOREEN: They say you get in for sure, and if you don't there be no more Department so no more houses, or clinics, or store... I hear womans talkin' yes'dy.

O'CONNOR: That's very interesting, Doreen. Maybe we can help your boyfriend. [*He goes to his case, extracts a bottle of whisky and two mugs.*] He didn't want to come here with you, I gather.

DOREEN: He a bit sick, in the hospital. He comin' out tomorrow.

O'CONNOR: Have a drink, Doreen. 'Hot stuff' as you say here, eh?

DOREEN: [*taking it*] Hot stuff make my head go real funny.

O'CONNOR: Mine too. Cheers.

He swallows, she sips.

I could try and get your boyfriend a job, Doreen. If you promised to do me a favour.

She nods.

It's very important in the next six months that I hear what people are doing on this Reserve.

DOREEN: I don't know very much, I's just ordinary girl. Missus Jenny Bob be more better for sure, she know everything.

O'CONNOR: An ordinary girl is just what I want, someone who can tell me the... silly little things that happen. Why don't you call me Uncle Bernie?

DOREEN: What silly things... Uncle Bernie?

O'CONNOR: Ohh, if there were strange people on the Reserve, people you'd never seen before. Or, if you saw someone putting up papers like mine with another face on it. You could tell me when I came up again who was doing things like that, and I could bring you presents. Would you like that?

She nods and sips.

And if you really want a nice present, you could tear down those papers with other faces. In the night when no one's looking.

Lydia Miller as Doreen and Raymond Blanco as O'Connor in the 1989 Toe Truck Theatre production. (Photo: Chooi Tan)

DOREEN: What sort of presents you bring, Uncle Bernie?

O'CONNOR: Anything you want. I'll give you a little one now. I always carry a few for... contingencies.

DOREEN: Con what?

O'CONNOR: Never mind. Close your eyes. Go on, close them.

> *She closes her eyes as he moves to his case. He takes out a small vinyl pouch with zipper. He unzips this and holds the pouch in front of her.*

DOREEN: Can I stop closin' my eyes now?

O'CONNOR: After three. One, two, three.

DOREEN: [*opening her eyes*] Make-up. Lipstick. Eye shadow. This is... mascara.

O'CONNOR: That's some rouge for your cheeks.

DOREEN: No, it's blusher.

O'CONNOR: Have another hot stuff.

> *He pours.*

DOREEN: I better not.

O'CONNOR: Do you good. Put hair on your chest. I'll bring you something even better than make-up next time.

DOREEN: I reckon election business pretty important, eh, Uncle Bernie...?

> *She applies blusher.*

O'CONNOR: It's very important. Some candidates want to separate black people from white. They want to put the Aborigines on separate land. That's what land rights means. Here, let me hold the mirror for you.

> *She starts to apply the eye shadow.*

Have you heard of South Africa, Doreen?

DOREEN: Africa, yes.

O'CONNOR: In one part of Africa black people are separate from white. This is called apartheid. This is very bad for black people. In Queensland, that is what these Labor people want, and what these troublemakers of the Land Rights Committee are after. But the National Party government and my Department believe in integration.

Jim Holt as O'Connor and Trisha Morton-Thomas as Doreen in the 1999 Riverina Theatre Company production. (Photo: Lee Verrall)

DOREEN: Integration.

O'CONNOR: Yes. That looks good.

DOREEN: I's lookin' like Hollywood already.

O'CONNOR: Put some mascara on now. [*He pours again while holding the mirror.*] White people should be mates with black people so they can be integrated. A lot of black men and women are a little bit white already. You've got some white blood, haven't you, Doreen?

DOREEN: I got some for sure. Some men from a boat took my gran'ma 'way when she a girl and…

O'CONNOR: No need to tell me the details.

DOREEN: I got a lot of white grandfathers, I reckon.

O'CONNOR: That looks very pretty. Can I put your lipstick on for you? I have a niece, you know. I often used to help her with her make-up.

DOREEN: I maybe better go.

O'CONNOR: I'm Uncle Bernie, Doreen. You'd let your uncle help you, wouldn't you? Wouldn't you?

> DOREEN *nods.*

My Department wants black and white to be together. But these troublemakers want separation. They want to throw boomerangs and wear no clothes.

> *He applies lipstick.*

Would you like to wear no clothes, Doreen?

DOREEN: No.

O'CONNOR: Of course not. Most Aborigines look terrible with nothing on, anyway. Mind you, I could look at you with no clothes on. Indeed I could.

> *He strokes her thigh.*

DOREEN: You talk a bit like one a' my white gran'fathers.

O'CONNOR: What do you mean?

DOREEN: He wanna love me when I was young girl. I tol' him his bad man to do this. Bad thing, I reckon.

O'CONNOR: Well yes, it can be.

DOREEN: You are not like him. You are good. You are a good man.

She stares at him expectantly. After some seconds he takes his hand off her and breaks away.

You see. You are good.

O'CONNOR: Yes, Doreen. Yes... Men get lonely sometimes. When a man travels a lot, he loses some of his good part. You see, I don't have any love with my wife anymore... so...

DOREEN: But you still marry.

O'CONNOR: Yes.

DOREEN: You livin' in your nice house together, but you got no love. No love left?

O'CONNOR: That's right. It's the whitefella's way.

DOREEN: I's very sorry, Uncle Bernie.

O'CONNOR: So am I.

DOREEN: I got to help my boyfriend to be good. I do election things for you and you be gettin' him a jobs so he can make money to buy a tickets for us to Brissie. We go way from Cheka so he not be fightin' no more.

O'CONNOR: Just so I remember, I'm putting it into my diary. What's his name?

DOREEN: Eddie Thomas... What's wrong?

O'CONNOR: Nothing. Nothing. [*He writes.*] Job... for... Eddie Thomas. I'll speak to the manager tomorrow.

DOREEN: You a real good man, Uncle Bernie... I gotta go now, I reckon.

O'CONNOR: Look Doreen, don't tell anyone about tonight, will you? Don't tell Eddie or Jenny Bob.

DOREEN: Eddie kill me if he fine out I bin try help him. But if I don't he'll never get a jobs and he'll never stop fightin'.

O'CONNOR: Doreen. If you tell me lots of those silly things when I come back next month, I'll give you a really special present. I'll give you that ticket to fly to Brisbane. How would you like that?

DOREEN: You kiddin' me...?

O'CONNOR: No.

DOREEN: Me in Brisbane?

O'CONNOR: Yes.

DOREEN: You real good whitefella, I reckon. But I gotta go with my Eddie.

O'CONNOR: I'll get a ticket for him too.

> *She yelps.*

Wait a minute… If you tell me a lot more silly things the next time after that.

DOREEN: So in two months we gunna have two tickets to Brissie?

> *He nods.*

O'CONNOR; But you're not to tell anyone about the tickets, not even Eddie, or about the silly things you tell me. And you mustn't tell anyone where you got that make-up case. Okay?

DOREEN: 'Course not. It'll be the secret of Doreen and… Uncle Bernie.

SCENE SIX

Backyard of JENNY BOB's *house. Daytime.* EDDIE *has his arm in a sling.* JENNY BOB *is sorting through mail. He takes his arm out of the sling to examine his hand.*

JENNY: Put that arm back inside. Now. Time you started doing as you're told 'round here. I don't want no trouble from you while you are sick, do you hear me?

> *He grunts. She puts the mail down.*

What good does it do to shoot yourself, Eddie? You make me 'nother ten years older when you do such things. I must be two hundred by now. Best place for you inside that hospital, I'd say, lying flat out and tied up with those tubes and bottles. How much blood they stick inside you?

EDDIE: Coupla flagons, I reckon. I got another man inside me now.

JENNY: Manager was very cross with you. They had to wake him up to tell him you shot yourself.

EDDIE: I thought that'd make him happy.

JENNY: What's in your ear?

EDDIE: Nothin'. [*He moves away from her.*] Doctor check me out and found a bit a' trouble in there.

Raymond Blanco as Eddie and Lydia Miller as Mrs Jenny Bob in the 1989 Toe Truck Theatre production. (Photo: Chooi Tan)

JENNY: You had that ever since you were a little bloke. It still hurting, eh?

EDDIE: Bit. I get somethin' loud inside my head. Like horses. It so loud it hurt me sometimes.

JENNY: You got to rest, my boy. You got to stop this drinking and running around like a rooster. You got to stop till you out of that bandage. I'm going to make sure you sit around here with us old chooks doing nothing.

EDDIE: You doin' nothing? You the busiest chook I ever seen.

She laughs and picks up an envelope.

JENNY: Eddie.

She indicates the seat. He sits.

I want you to promise your gran'ma something.

EDDIE: What?

JENNY: I want you to promise to stay sitting down when you finish reading this letter.

EDDIE: Why?

JENNY: Just promise.

EDDIE: What is it?

JENNY: Say, 'I promise to stay on my seat…'

EDDIE: I promise. Pass it over.

JENNY: '… by the Holy Bible and Jesus Christ.'

EDDIE: Yeah. Give us it.

JENNY: Say it.

EDDIE: By the Bible… and Jesus. Gissit.

She extracts a document from the envelope, unfolds it and passes it to him. He reads it.

Fuckin' court!

JENNY: You promised to sit down. By the Bible. Sit!

He sits.

You taken the wrong car this time. Mister Tomkins from the company.

EDDIE: What's up with him? I didn't leave one scratch on that car. Even left the radio in it.

JENNY: He said he had to drive his wife's little car for two days and that made him very angry.

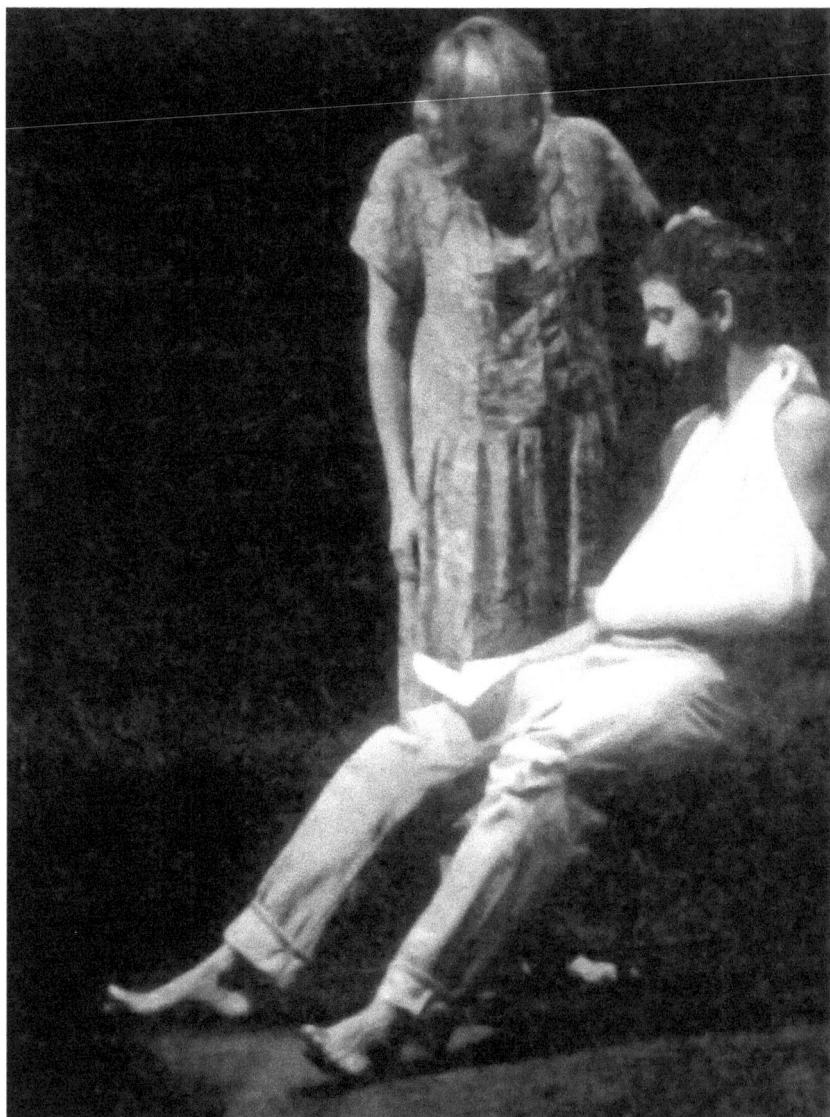

Trisha Morton-Thomas as Mrs Jenny Bob and Lee Willis as Eddie in the 1999 Riverina Theatre Company production. (Photo: Lee Verrall)

EDDIE: They can't send me to Stuart again. Gran, you gotta talk to this man.

JENNY: I already done that. I told him you were sorry. He said the company was sick of cars being stolen by young Aborigines. He said a lot of other things about us too.

EDDIE: They bastards, Gran'ma. They're fuckin' bastards.

JENNY: I know, child.

EDDIE: I want my own car. I want to work, but they give me shit jobs. I try to be friendly. I say 'Hello' to them but they just look the other way… foreman, company blokes, even the fuckin' truck drivers. I wear this black skin in that white town like it's a bright light. I dig a ditch for their new tree in the middle of their fuckin' town and I can see 'em smilin' and thinkin', 'Another one digging a black hole for himself', and I dig, Gran'ma, and I want to dig deeper and deeper, till I disappear.

JENNY: Come here, boy.

She holds him in her arms.

I know you are good in your heart, and that you have a love for your people. Doreen knows too. And your mum and dad know, even when they are fighting. Your little brother, he talks about you all the time; about how you teach him to hunt for bandicoot and dive for fish. And your sisters think you are a big strong man and are very proud of you when they see you at Yambala, hunting, tracking and looking after our country. These other people don't matter, these paper people. But we do, your own people do, and your own land. You must think about this, Eddie.

SCENE SEVEN

Night-time. EDDIE*'s bedroom* DOREEN *watches as* EDDIE *drinks from a wine cask. He throws the cask at her.*

EDDIE: You was laughin' with him over the canteen. I saw youse.

DOREEN: I laughin' with everyones. They all our mob. You just angry 'bout court tomorrow. We all be there to help…

EDDIE: He was lookin' at you too. I seen. You fucked him when I was down in gaol, didn't y'?

DOREEN: I didn't.

EDDIE: Now you want him again.

> *He takes out his hunting knife and holds it against the inside of his forearm.*

DOREEN: No more, Eddie, don't do this. I bin tell you fella so many time I's never been near him. I only had husband, that's all.

> EDDIE *drags the flat edge of the knife dangerously along his arm.*

EDDIE: You lyin', you fuckin' lyin'. You want him.

DOREEN: Eddie, that not true. You're my man. I'm belong you, no one else for me.

EDDIE: What's he got, bitch?

DOREEN: Eddie, Eddie, please don't do this 'gain.

EDDIE: He's got a job, has he? Like that, do y'?

DOREEN: Give me knife now, Eddie. I give it back tomorrow, promise.

EDDIE: Fuck off.

> *As he scrapes the knife along his arm,* DOREEN *tries to stop him. He shoves her.*

Go fuck your Islander.

DOREEN: I don't like him, Eddie. I just loves you.

EDDIE: Yeah? Yeah? Just me, eh? Just me? Just me? Just me? [*He pulls a crumpled airline ticket from his pocket.*] What's this, then? What's this I found in your bag? What's this ticket for Brisbane?

DOREEN: That's not from him, Eddie.

EDDIE: Yeah? Then why you bin hide it, bitch?

DOREEN: It from Mister O'Connor, the Director.

EDDIE: Liar!

DOREEN: He tell me it's big secret. He tol' me he gunna get one for you too.

EDDIE: You lyin' bitch!

DOREEN: No, Eddie. I's hidin' my ticket till yours come next month and—

EDDIE: [*interrupting*] You fuckin' lyin' cunt. Islander buy you a
    ticket to Brisbane, then Sydney, Melbourne—
DOREEN: No, this not true.
EDDIE: You go all the way with him.
DOREEN: No, Eddie—Give me this knife.

> *She grabs his arm.*

I just got love for you, Eddie.
EDDIE: Just me, eh? What's this? What's this? What's this?

> *He comes at her with the ticket and knife.*

DOREEN: No knife, Eddie. Had that already from husband. No knife!
EDDIE: You fuck with anyone!
DOREEN: No!
EDDIE: Yes! I seen your eyes for him, and now I seen your ticket,
    you *slut!*
DOREEN: Eddie, I loves—

> *He shouts as he lunges and drives the knife into her ribs. She
> falls. He stares at her for some time, then walks in a circle
> around her. He stops and kneels beside her, touches her face
> tenderly. He still holds the ticket in the other hand.*

EDDIE: Doreen, Doreen… Doreen. Doreen. Come on, you talk to me
    now, Doreen. Talk to your Eddie, eh, Doreen… I'm listen now.
    I'm okay. You talk, eh Doreen?

> *He takes her hand and strokes it.*

Why you don't talk? You little bit sick, eh? I take you to gran,
she watchin' tellie. She look after y'.

> *He picks her up tenderly.*

MAN: He carried his girl to Jenny Bob's. His gran'ma was sitting in
    the flickering grey light of the TV. Eddie laid Doreen on the
    floor and walked off into the night.

> *The MAN lets the WOMAN down onto her feet. They both face
> the audience.*

WOMAN: 'Someone there? That you, Eddie?'
MAN: Jenny Bob looked over her shoulder and saw Doreen on the
    floor.

WOMAN: 'I'm not lifting a finger to help you, girl. If you going to go down that canteen with Eddie then you got to look after yourself. I see you when you sober, and not before.'

MAN: An hour or so later she went to the fridge.

WOMAN: The light from the fridge spilled across the floor. And Jenny Bob saw Doreen's blood.

END OF ACT ONE

Lee Willis as Eddie and Trisha Morton-Thomas as Doreen in the 1999 Riverina Theatre Company production. (Photo: Lee Verrall)

ACT TWO

SCENE ONE

Stuart Prison, Townsville. Day. The LAWYER *enters* EDDIE*'s cell. He holds up a bulging string bag.*

LAWYER: Oranges. [*He drops them on the floor.*] They tell me you've given up salt, sugar and tobacco. [*Pause.*] The bad news is, the Government won't give us any funds for your case. In fact they're annoyed we want to do it. The good news is, we've decided to push ahead anyway. We've already sent one of our lawyers to talk to reserve councils. And the Aboriginal Legal Service has agreed to collect information on past cases going back twenty years. We've even persuaded two students here in Townsville to spend their spare time in the library researching for the case. And me? Thanks to you, I've flown out of here twice already with a briefcase bulging with information, eh mate? My boss is blown away by all the help you've been giving. Ecstatic he is. [*Pause.*] You've had your thinking time, Eddie. Now it's time to talk. Talk, Eddie. [*Pause.*] Fuck, eh? [*Pause.*] You're up on first degree, mate. They're out to get you, to put you in a box like this for life. Understand? But the Public Defender's Office is going to spend months working on your case to show everyone in this country the full story of reserve life, about Yambala and about the troubles and feelings inside you. We think that reserves are wrong for Aboriginal people and that you wouldn't have killed if your life had been better…

He waits for an answer.

Or maybe you would have anyway, eh? Maybe you're a mad fucking boong who can't think, can't talk and ought to spend the rest of his life in a cage…

EDDIE: I killed my woman. I must die.

LAWYER: You die and you'll help no one. If you live you can help your people. [*Pause.*] I've sent a letter to your grandmother. Maybe she'll know how to get through to you.

EDDIE: She given up on me.

> *The* LAWYER *prepares to leave.*

LAWYER: Today you've spoken. I'm happy about that. Really happy.

> *He exits.*

SCENE TWO

The Reserve at night. The visitors' house. O'CONNOR *is at the window throwing lollies and drinking.*

O'CONNOR: Hey, kids! That's it! Here's a big one…! Let's see who's the strongest.

> *He throws the 'big one', waves, then catches sight of someone to one side.*

Missus Jenny Bob. Come in, come in.

JENNY: [*entering*] I don't like you throwing lollies to the children.

O'CONNOR: You've said that before. Better lollies than sniffing petrol. So-o-o. How's the grandson? Comfortable down there in Stuart, is he? [*Pause.*] Cat got your tongue?

JENNY: Why have you called me here, Director?

O'CONNOR: There's a rumour about.

JENNY: Which one's that?

O'CONNOR: That you've agreed to sit on the Cape York Land Rights Committee.

JENNY: This is not your concern.

O'CONNOR: Everything on this Reserve and every reserve in the State is my concern.

JENNY: You must allow us to do our own business, Director.

O'CONNOR: You people have never been able to do your own business… and I don't think you ever will. I've been around this State long enough to know that.

Jim Holt as the Lawyer and Lee Willis as Eddie in the 1999 Riverina Theatre Company production. (Photo: Lee Verrall)

Lydia Miller as Mrs Jenny Bob and Raymond Blanco as O'Connor in the 1989 Toe Truck Theatre production. (Photo: Chooi Tan)

JENNY: Your tongue moving too much for your own good, Director.

O'CONNOR: You just can't cope with the whitefella's way. Look, look. When I was a young bloke I visited a mission with my father, Dad, and you know what? Listen to this: all the blacks around this mission had been tamed, all except this blackfella called Potato. Potato lived in the bush and kept to himself; wouldn't come near the station. No one could catch him, not the missionaries, the police or the local government officers. And do you know why they couldn't, Jenny Bob? Do you know why? Because he kept himself covered from head to foot in his own shit. That's head to foot. No one'd touch the bastard. Fact... This Land Rights Committee, Jenny Bob, they're just like that fella Potato.

JENNY: How much you been drinking?

O'CONNOR: You inferring I'm drunk?

JENNY: You are drunk. I don't want to talk to you in this state.

O'CONNOR: You talk to your own people when they're pissed.

JENNY: But you are Director, and candidate for Parliament.

He lifts his drink.

O'CONNOR: To the National Party of Queensland.

JENNY: National Party stinks like your crap.

O'CONNOR *nearly chokes on his drink.*

O'CONNOR: Well, well. Feeling our oats at sixty-five, are we? Who's tongue's wagging now? You listen to me, Missus Jenny Chairlady Bob: you're sacked from the Cheka Aboriginal Council, as of now. Due to approaching senility. You stupid old gin.

JENNY: When you going to wake up? We're not going to put you in Parliament. You think black people are stupid. But we laugh at you. We laugh when we see you marching 'round here in your safari suit. We laugh because you are a fool.

O'CONNOR: How dare you talk to me like that. You better vote for me or I'll have the lot of you crawling for your crust. And if I hear you've been stirring up anti-National Party trouble here, I'll move your whole family off Yambala and I'll make sure they never go back. Never. Understand? [*He drinks.*] You're out of your depth in this game, old woman. You've been a thorn in my side for years with your non-stop nagging about our shortcomings, when you can't even keep your own house in order. Look at your family: a daughter who's a bludging hypochondriac, a useless son-in-law whose only skill is croc shooting and bending his elbow, and two alcoholic murderers for grandsons. Who have I left out? I'm sure they're just the tip of the iceberg. Any other close relatives I haven't heard about? Eh?

JENNY: There are many. But I will tell you of only one. My sister on Batavia Downs outstation.

O'CONNOR: Well, you've got a sister on Batavia. What's she? A crippled diabetic with incurable ulcers?

JENNY: She got trachoma, Mister O'Connor. Stage four.

O'CONNOR: Now hold on, hold on a minute. Don't you go blaming me for that...

JENNY: You and the Premier the ones who cancelled the Trachoma Program three years ago.

O'CONNOR: We did that because those medical officers were telling tribal blacks to vote Labor.

JENNY: No, Director. They were telling people how to vote.

O'CONNOR: Same thing.

JENNY: My sister cannot see my face anymore. She can't see the trees or dust from the kangaroos. When she looks up, she can't see the clouds like white camels walking across the blue sky. No, Director. My sister doesn't see the sun sinking into the sea at Yambala. It's night all the time for her now. You can see these things, Director, but you are blind too. You sold my family and my people for thirty pieces of silver when you took us from Yambala twenty years ago, and three years ago you sold my sister's eyes.

O'CONNOR: Look, I'm sorry about that, Missus Bob. Why didn't you tell me about her at the time?

JENNY: I told you.

O'CONNOR: Not about your sister, you didn't.

JENNY: No. I talked for all outstation people. But you didn't listen. The same as you bring in new Aboriginal Act of Parliament every few years and don't listen to blacks. You know better what we need. You knew better when the boat took us from our country. You knew better when you got the company to build us these boxes and straight roads.

Trisha Morton-Thomas as Mrs Jenny Bob and Jim Holt as O'Connor in
the 1999 Riverina Theatre Company production. (Photo: Lee Verrall)

O'CONNOR: Jenny Bob, I can't listen to everyone's advice.

JENNY: I have talked for so many years to you for improvement in our lives, but you never change, because you are empty inside. Why you shaking your head, Director? You got something inside, you got a belief? Do you believe in Jesus Christ? No. You believe in your family? Maybe your wife. But I see no love for woman in your eyes. You believe in your Parliament? Or this British justice? I don't think so. What about the land? Aaah, yes. Yes, you believe in the land, don't you? Make a hole in it here, dig up over there, take the oil or bauxite, then put the money in the bank and finish with it. [*Pause.*] This land is bleeding, Director. You cut into the body, pull out the bones and leave the bleeding flesh. This Cape York land cries out. I have heard it.

O'CONNOR: Missus Bob.

JENNY: Yes, Director.

O'CONNOR: Could you… go. Please.

JENNY: I will go if you tell me the thing you believe in.

O'CONNOR: I… can't think… I…

JENNY: Must be one thing. Must be.

> O'CONNOR *has trouble breathing. He stumbles to his suitcase, opens it and rummages for his bottle. As he drinks,* JENNY BOB *notices something in amongst his clothing. Unnoticed, she picks up a plastic make-up case identical to* DOREEN*'s.*

I see what it is you believe in, Director. I see why you have given twenty years to black people.

> *He sees the make-up case in her hand.*

Did Doreen like your present very much, Director?

O'CONNOR: I can explain that. Yes, I gave one of those to her when she came 'round to beg for a job for Eddie. It's true. It's even in my diary. I'll—

JENNY: [*interrupting*] You are a snake who spoils young girls. It is true, these stories I have heard. You have used black girls like you use other people in your politics. Use what's sweet inside, then throw away the packet.

O'CONNOR: I didn't do that. Missus Bob… believe me…

JENNY: You give your lollies when they are kids, then make-up when they are girls, and then something else when they women. I understand this ticket now. [*She holds up* DOREEN's *crumpled airline ticket.*] I found it on the floor where Doreen died. A ticket with her name to Brisbane. I understand now, Uncle Bernie!

O'CONNOR: Please, Jenny Bob, I didn't touch Doreen. I didn't, I swear it…

JENNY: If you didn't spoil her, why did you give her this ticket? [*Shouting*] Why did you give her this ticket?

O'CONNOR: I… I asked her to tell me… things about the Reserve, about what people were saying about the election. I said I would send her a ticket so she could go to Brisbane.

JENNY: You asked a young girl to spy on her own people and then you spoiled her! And you sent her this ticket to Brisbane so you could meet with her and spoil her again!

O'CONNOR: No, no. I didn't, I didn't!

JENNY: You are a mongrel.

O'CONNOR: You must believe me; why don't you believe me?

JENNY: How can I believe a filthy mongrel who cannot feel, who cannot weep. Weep if you have any feeling for her.

O'CONNOR: I would. I would…

JENNY: But you can't. No. You cannot even weep, while our own people cut themselves for their dead. Our people bleed, while you cannot weep. How can I believe such a man as you?

O'CONNOR: I give you my word.

JENNY: Your word is worth nothing at all to me. I am going.

> *She moves towards the door.*

O'CONNOR: I could cut myself. I could.

> *She stops. He grabs a packet of razors from his toilet bag and takes one out. He holds it over his forearm, looking at her.*

You see, I could cut myself too.

JENNY: Could you, Director?

O'CONNOR: I could cut. I could bleed.

> *She turns and exits. He looks after her and calls.*

I could. I could. I could…

Lydia Miller as Mrs Jenny Bob in the 1989 Toe Truck Theatre
production. (Photo: Chooi Tan)

SCENE THREE

Prison cell. Daytime. JENNY BOB *enters and stands looking at* EDDIE. *He turns away.*

JENNY: You wondering where your grandmother been, eh?... She been sitting in her broken-down old chair outside her little house, thinking. Six weeks. That old chair just held onto me, Eddie, wouldn't let go. I talk to it, I say, 'My grandson, he's in Stuart Prison, I got to go down and see him.' And the chair say to me, say, 'That grandson of yours, he's no good; he kill beautiful girl, a girl he loved.' 'That don't matter,' I say, 'He's down there in that prison, no one to help him, no one to talk to him.' But still that old chair don't let go of me. 'He just another one drank too much and kill his own family', it says. 'Hundreds like him all over this State, this year, year before, next year... Forget him', says my chair.

    EDDIE *turns to look at her.*

But it's hard to forget, boy; hard to forget you are part of me, no matter what happens... Six weeks I was sitting like this. Then I got a letter from the court people in Brisbane. And I showed that old chair the letter. That chair put on its glasses and it read what the court people wanted to do. It saw that they wanted to find out all about your case so everyone can understand properly about all this killing, and about reserves and about Yambala, our country. This letter said, 'We want to know Eddie's story.' And you know what? That old chair, it thought a little while, and then it let go of me at last... And I got on the Fokker Friendship and come to see my grandson.

    EDDIE *rises, goes to her and is enfolded.*

EDDIE: Gran'ma.

JENNY: I hope you have some forgiveness for an old woman. [*Pause.*] They say you don't talk to anyone here. [*Pause.*] You must stop thinking of what has gone before, and start to think of the future.

EDDIE: I must be punished.

JENNY: You have had so much punishment already, and you will bear much more. You must talk to the court people.

EDDIE: I hate court, Gran'ma.

JENNY: No one likes courts, not even those that made them, child. But your case is very important for all Aboriginal people.

EDDIE: How?

JENNY: I will show you… Remember when you were small in Cheka and I would put you on my back and fly you back over our own country?

EDDIE: Over Yambala.

JENNY: And I would show you the special trees, the hills, the rocks and the waterholes? Remember that?

EDDIE: Yes, and you ran 'round and 'round, and we put our hands out like them wild geese.

JENNY: Today we're going on flying trip over this place they call Queensland. You want to come?

EDDIE: I want to, Gran'ma, I want to.

JENNY: But not on my back. You're too big now. This time you just put your hand on my shoulder. There. Now, off we go.

She dips her body as though shooting into the air.

Off we go, little one, up from Stuart Prison, up into the sky.

EDDIE: Yes, Gran'ma, yes.

JENNY: Now we will see this Land of the Queen properly… Plenty of wind as we fly over the Townsville suburbs down there, over city park with our people camping under date palms, up the coast past Palm Island Reserve out there in the sea, to Yarrabah, Herberton and half dozen other reserves inland. See them? Now up to Cairns and you can see your brothers in the park by the sea, drinking metho and putting their noses in the petrol tin…

EDDIE: I see them. They wavin'.

JENNY: But not the older men with them. They can't see us.

EDDIE: Trachoma.

JENNY: Oyster beds in their eyes. We heading over Mossman now, and Daintree, Bloomfield.

EDDIE: Reserves everywhere, Gran'ma.

JENNY: And they all got their manager, office, their square houses and their straight roads...

EDDIE: Blackfella never make road like that.

JENNY: Now, up we go, up, up so we can see much more, all the islands running to Papua New Guinea. You see Cheka right over there?

EDDIE: So far away, Gran'ma... I see it, but. One dot for Cheka town and smaller one for Cheka Reserve.

JENNY: We go down closer. I see Mister O'Connor shooting ducks over at the lagoon with the company man, Mister Tomkins.

EDDIE: Hope they shoot each other up the bum.

JENNY: And you can see Doreen's mum from here. Coughing up blood in the drum behind her house.

EDDIE: Yeh.

JENNY: Now we fly down to Aurukun.

EDDIE: Then to Dajarra, Boulia, Birdsville, across to Eulo.

JENNY: And fast across nice square whitefella farms to the coast.

EDDIE: Surfers Paradise, Gran'ma. Why they call it paradise?

JENNY: Because this is where white people come when they are dead. Now you see Brisbane coming up.

EDDIE: Go that way to them big buildings.

JENNY: What for?

EDDIE: I want to piss on the Premier's roof.

JENNY: What a naughty boy. We going over Musgrave Park now, and you can see the police picking up people because they got no keys.

EDDIE: No fixed address.

JENNY: No fixed address, so into the paddy wagon. Now we heading over Cherbourg, in the Premier's electorate.

EDDIE: It looks a bit better 'n ours.

JENNY: Got to be, boy. That's the one they take the TV cameras and important people to... We going inland a bit so you can catch a look at all the reserves: Zamia Creek, Woorabinda, Duaringa, Foleyvale, and Rockhampton with its hostel for Aborigines over there. And we keep going...

EDDIE: I see Townsville 'gain.

JENNY: Yes.

EDDIE: Hey, you goin' straight back to Stuart.

JENNY: Have to.

EDDIE: But I like it up here with you.

JENNY: We got to come down to earth sometime, child. Down we go, through the clouds. Look down and you see all sorts of ants walking in Stuart Prison.

EDDIE: Most of them is black ants, eh Gran'ma.

JENNY: Down to the window, and we go through the bars into your cell.

She makes the action of landing.

You see now why you got to talk in court?

He nods.

These things you see from the sky got to be changed. It is your job now. You must talk to these whitefellers so they know the truth. And when the case is finished you will work for your people, till one day you can take your grandmother, your mum and dad and brothers and sisters on your shoulders for flying trip over a better place.

He holds her arm.

EDDIE: I will.

She prepares to leave.

Gran'ma, somethin' been troubling me. A long time. Somethin' in my head.

JENNY: What is it, child?

EDDIE: It's a dream. At night. I got to ask you 'bout it.

JENNY: Tell me this dream.

EDDIE: Horses. Horses chase me at night when I sleep. They frighten me because they are so loud in my ears.

JENNY: Are there many horses?

EDDIE: Maybe ten, or twelve. They all different colours, I think. The one out front, it's a big red horse... I remember now. It's got white socks on its legs, and when it chase me I run to an old man tree with a mark in his chest.

JENNY: Eddie. Your gran'pa told you a story. You forgot.

EDDIE: Tell me the story again, Gran'ma.

JENNY: No point in you knowing this, Eddie.

EDDIE: I want to know it. I'm sick of this galloping that nearly blows up my head. I gotta know. Tell me, Gran'ma.

   Pause.

JENNY: It is a story of children, long time ago. You see, one morning they went off from camp to look for Blue Emperor butterflies. They were out quite a while and they saw all kinds, but couldn't find a blue one at all. Then the eldest boy saw one bigger than anything from his dreams. He shouted to the others and they all chased the Blue Emperor till they reached a big lagoon. The butterfly went here, then there, to all the bushes and flowers 'round the water's edge. They sat watching it for a long time and they were very happy. Then they heard a noise like thunder. It came closer and closer, and the eldest told the other children to get ready for the rain. They all looked up in the sky, but nothing. Then they saw a man on a big horse with white legs galloping through the trees and a dozen others coming behind. These men on their horses galloped straight into the children. The oldest boy rolled into the water and he watched as the bones of his brothers and sisters and cousins cracked and broke under the horse's legs. He lay very still in the water as the blood of his family flowed into the lagoon all around him, the blood of those eight little children. The man on the red horse took out his knife and cut his initials and a big number eight in an old tree by the water's edge. There are many trees like this in our country.

EDDIE: I remember now, Gran'ma. I remember Gran'pa tellin' me about the white socks of that horse turning red, and that man laughing as he galloped away. An' that Blue Emperor came down on top of the kids and it died too. I seen that tree. Old man silver gum with mark on his chest. I been to that place.

   Pause.

JENNY: Your gran'pa saw all that. He came out of that lagoon and lay down for three days. His legs couldn't carry him away.

   She pats his hand.

We are all children of that red lagoon. You found your story now. You will never forget. [*She stands.*] Time for me to go. Goodbye, my boy.

She walks to the periphery of the cell, stops for a moment and looks back.

EDDIE: Gran'ma…

The MAN *and* WOMAN *face the audience. The* MAN *holds an exercise book.*

MAN: He talked to the lawyers. He told them all the things he could remember about his life. Many people worked for more than a year to get the case ready. He had to learn patience, eh? Good people spoke at his trial. He was surprised. They got down all sorts of top people from the universities. His own family got up in this big Brisbane court with no windows and told everyone things about his life. It mixed his stomach up a lot, I can tell you. When the trial ended, the judge said he should get parole straight away. But then he didn't get out right away. The Parole Board was trying to find a place he could go to learn something. While he was waiting, he had a chance to read all the newspaper stories about the trial and that was a shock. And he started reading books for the first time. [*Pause.*] They sent him to a station up the Atherton Tableland where he got the hang of riding and breaking-in… horses, that is. He liked it up there. He was still drinking a fair bit, so after a while he went to Brisbane to a drying-out place called Jodara. They had a AA program going. After a couple of months, he was doing okay, and started being chairman of some AA meetings… a chairman, just like his gran'ma. He didn't feel like fighting people anymore. That was a big change. That's when he started writing. In these schoolbooks. Poems and songs. And he started learning guitar and playing for some of the other fellas in the place. He was shy, but he could lose himself in the music, eh?

WOMAN: He would like to return to his own land and work for his people, but he doesn' want to go back up there if it will cause trouble for Doreen's family. He would like the land that was taken from his people when he was a child to be given back. We need the land so we can take our own road to the future.

The MAN *becomes* EDDIE *as he opens the exercise book.*

EDDIE: Give back the earth my father knew,
           Give back the bones my grandfather heard,
           Give back the land of our secrets and legends
           Whose lessons hide in flower stalks
           And river stones.
           Give back,
           And we will be free
           And there will be peace.

He lifts his hand and opens his palm. In it is the river stone
DOREEN *gave him. He stares at it.*

THE END

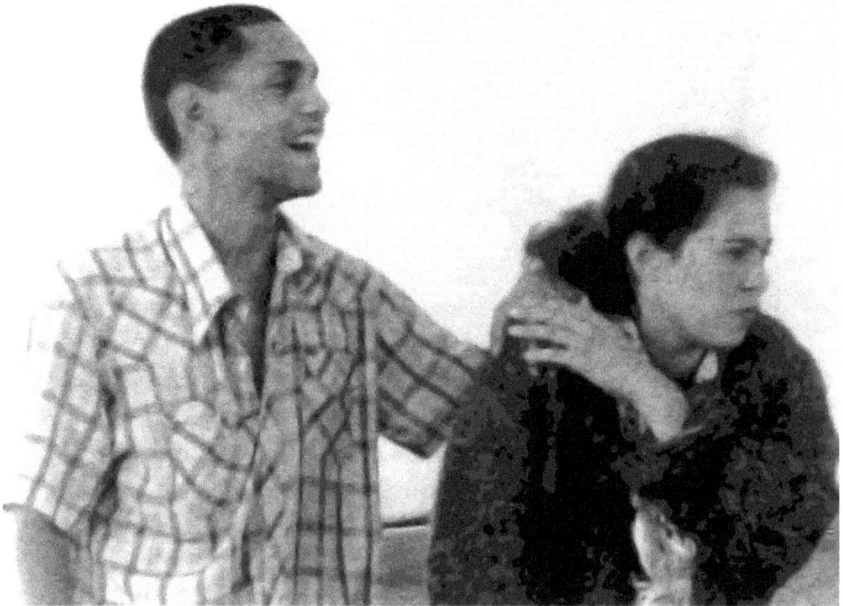

Raymond Blanco as Eddie and Lydia Miller as Mrs Jenny Bob in the 1989
Toe Truck Theatre production. (Photo: Chooi Tan)

www.ingramcontent.com/pod-product-compliance
Lightning Source LLC
Chambersburg PA
CBHW041934090426
42744CB00017B/2053